Dedicated to my mother,
Susan DelSignore Howes

My Grandma Rose: Alzheimer's and Dementia from a Middle Schooler's Perspective

by Kim Roman
Illustrated by Nataly Vits

Chapter 1

Me and My Family:

Hi Everyone!

My name is Carly and I want to tell you about my family. Hopefully, if you're going through something similar, this book will help you. Let me start by telling you about me and my family. I'm 12 years old, my brother Jake is 11, and there's also my mom and dad. But this story is really about my Grandma Rose who died last year. She had Alzheimer's Disease, and as the years went by, she forgot more and more things. It was very sad and sometimes scary, and I'm just now able to talk about it without crying.

My brother and I are glad our parents told us the truth, but I'm not going to lie to you, it was hard to go through. Before they told us what was wrong, we were really scared and thought it might be our fault that Grandma went through this. You know, we often feel that we are responsible for what happens in our families – whether our parents are going through a divorce, or if one of them drinks too much. Or even if they have a medical problem.

Please don't think that you are responsible for these things. There is so much that goes on around us that no one can control and most of the time it's not anyone's fault – things just happen and we have to learn how to cope with what's going on in our lives. We have to learn how to love our families and friends while they are with us. You never know when they might not be here anymore.

When bad things happen, there are adults in your life that can help you through these difficult times. Don't be afraid to ask for help or let your friends know how sad you are. You might want to go to your school counselor and tell them if you're having trouble sleeping, or are afraid or even just very sad.

You can also talk to your doctor about these things and they can get help for you. Of course you need to let your parents know how you are feeling. They will be sad too and you can help each other though these bad times.

My mom had a really tough time because Grandma Rose was her mother – it was hard to see my mom cry so much. She went to her doctor and he sent her to a specialist called a psychiatrist who helped her. It took a long time, but I'm glad she got help and encouraged me to talk to someone.

Jake had a particularly hard time after Grandma Rose died, but he reacted in an entirely different way. Instead of crying like Mom and I, he was angry all the time and yelled a lot. Dad said that everyone grieves in different ways and that's how Jake expressed himself. Thankfully that didn't last too long after he began talking to the school counselor.

It's very important not to keep your feelings inside. No matter who you choose, you really will feel better more quickly if you find some to talk to and share your thoughts and fears. Crying, wanting to be alone for a while and even anger are all normal ways people react when someone they care about is gone.

Did you know that there are seven stages of Alzheimer's Disease? Not everyone goes through them in the same amount of time or in the same way. It may help you to know about these stages and what your loved one might go through so that you can be prepared and even help them.

Chapter 2

Let's get back to Grandma Rose's story.

When we were very young Grandma used to take my brother and I to the park. We spent hours there playing on the swings and sliding down the slide. We giggled as we held tightly when she pushed us on the merry-go-round. We played hopscotch and run around having fun. I loved those carefree days.

I guess this is a good time to talk about what Alzheimer's Disease and other forms of dementia are. Alzheimer's is a type of dementia and there are a lot of reasons someone might have dementia.

All forms of dementia are brain conditions where someone has problems with memory and thinking.

Some people get dementia because they had a stroke or maybe they had a bad accident where they hit their head. Some people just get dementia.

You may hear strange new words like Alzheimer's, Parkinson's, Huntington's, Creutzfeldt-Jakob, Lewy Bodies -- all of these are types of dementia.

With all forms of dementia, one other word you'll probably hear is cognitive. That just means that it has something to do with the brain and remembering, making decisions, learning new things and concentrating.

For you, the type of dementia or the reason they get it doesn't matter. All you know is that someone you love is having problems and you want the doctors to be able to fix it.

Right now there isn't really anything the doctors can do, so what you can do for your loved one is to understand what they are going through and love them through it to the very end.

Stage 1: No Impairment – This means that you don't see any signs of dementia. Everything seems "normal".

Chapter 3

When Jake and I were about four and five years old, Grandma was going to take us to the park, but she couldn't find her car keys. We looked all over the house – under the sofa cushions, in her bedroom, her purse and even in the car, just in case she left it there the last time she drove. Instead of going to the park we walked around her neighborhood and played card games at her kitchen table. My brother asked for a glass of milk, and when Grandma opened the refrigerator, there were her keys!

We all had a good laugh about that. When Mom and Dad picked us up later we told them the story of the lost keys. Grandma, Jake and I laughed again. Mom looked at Dad and although they smiled, it didn't look like they thought it was as funny as we did. Dad looked back at Mom and shrugged his shoulders. At the time I didn't understand that this was a sign that something might be wrong with Grandma Rose.

Stage 2: Very Mild Decline – Your loved one might begin to notice that they are losing things and might just think this is a normal part of getting older.

If they are given a memory test, they will probably still do well and even their doctor might not realize that something is wrong.

Chapter 4

Every Friday evening Grandma Rose came to our house for dinner. Dad hadn't come home from work yet and Mom was in the kitchen cooking. She asked Grandma to read with us. I was seven and was getting pretty good at reading, but I loved snuggling on the sofa with Grandma and letting her read to us.

She made the stories come alive, using different voices for each character and acting the way she thought they would act. My brother was more fidgety and asked a lot of questions, but he loved snuggling with Grandma too.

We were reading our favorite story about elephants. Grandma had read it to us about a million times and she used to make funny animal sounds – trumpeting like an elephant, roaring like a lion, flapping her arms as if she were an ostrich.

This time she didn't do it. She just read the book – no funny noises, no acting out the parts. It wasn't as fun, but we still loved spending time with her.

Grandma had told us many times that elephants never forget. This time Jake asked her why elephants don't forget. She looked at him with a puzzled look on her face and said, "Where did you hear that?" Jake giggled and said, "Grandma, you told us." "I most certainly did not! I've never heard anything so ridiculous. Everyone forgets things," Grandma said angrily. "Even elephants!"

Mom quickly walked into the room, smiled and told the two of us to go wash our hands for dinner. That was the first time I had a bad feeling that something might be wrong with Grandma. Of course I didn't know what it was and I was afraid to talk about it.

We were only gone a short time, but when we got back, Dad was home, Grandma was in a better mood and everything was normal again. After dinner, Grandma Rose had to go home – she didn't like driving at night. My dad followed her out the door and said he needed to go to the store to get milk.

While he was gone, we got ready for bed and Mom read a story to us. "Why did Grandma Rose get mad at Jake for asking about the elephants," I asked? "Oh Sweetie, she wasn't mad at Jake. She was confused and frustrated.

"You may have noticed that she's been forgetting things lately. That can be normal as someone gets older, but we've just found out from her doctor that she probably has something called Alzheimer's Disease.

When you have a cold, you have symptoms like a fever or a cough. When someone has Alzheimer's or another form of dementia their symptoms are forgetting things and acting strangely."

A few minutes later Dad came home without any milk and told Mom that Grandma Rose had gotten home safely. He didn't really go to the store, he had followed her home. We all snuggled on the big sofa and talked.

Mom told us about how the brain works and reminded us how we love playing the matching game. When we were little we had cards with animals on one side -- there were two cards for each of the animals. The backs of the cards all looked the same so we had to try to remember where the animals were. We would turn over two of the cards. If they were the same, we had made a match and got to keep them. If they weren't the same, we had to flip them back over and try to remember what character was on the front of the cards.

At first we weren't very good at it, but after a lot of practice exercising our brains, we got better and better. Dad was really good at it and he used a regular deck of cards to play the game. Mom explained that as we get older, if we have dementia, instead of our brains getting better and better, they start to shrink and our memories get worse and worse.

She showed us some pamphlets from an organization that helps people with Alzheimer's and dementia. It was sad to know that unlike having a cold, Grandma Rose wasn't going to get better. Of course we knew that eventually everyone dies, our Grandpa Charlie had died before we were born, but this was very scary. Mom asked us how we were feeling – we were sad and scared and angry and confused.

"Grandma knows this is happening to her, and she's also sad and scared and angry and confused. She will need our love and support – no matter what, she's still your Grandma Rose. We'll talk more about this later, but you need to keep telling us how you are feeling – that's super important."

Stage 3: Mild Decline – This is the stage where people start noticing that something isn't quite right. This is also when their doctor begins to suspect they might have some form of cognitive problem.

This is the stage where they have trouble remembering words and planning their daily activities. They also have a harder time remembering the names of new people they are just meeting.

As you can see from Grandma Rose, this is also when they start losing things.

Chapter 5

When I was eight, we were at Grandma's house after school. Jake and I sat at her kitchen table doing our homework. I was having trouble with a math problem and Grandma reminded me that she used to work in a bank and was really good at math. She became confused with the new type of math and then she got frustrated and angry when she didn't understand the problems. I told her that I was going to work on something else.

Grandma was helping Jake with his spelling words when Dad came to pick us up. Jake broke his pencil in the middle of a word and Grandma asked Dad to get another one from her desk. When he got there he noticed some bills that were marked "Past Due" and "Final Notice".

That night Mom and Dad talked about the bills and I heard them say that Grandma couldn't stay on her own any more. The next morning, we started cleaning out the craft room and turned it into a cozy room for Grandma. We hung family pictures on the walls and brought the bed and other things from her house to make it more familiar to her. On top of her bed we put the beautiful quilt that she had made many years ago.

We thought that Grandma Rose would be happy to move in with us, but instead she was angry and cried a lot, "You're treating me like a baby. I'm an adult, you know. You can't make me stay here if I don't want to. I'm going to call the police and tell them that you're kidnapping me." Then she looked at me and said, "Emma! Help me. These people are trying to steal my car and they won't let me go back to my house." She had called me by my mother's name.

Mom had explained to us that this might happen, but I was still stunned. I told her it was going to be okay, but I wasn't so sure.

Then Mom gave me her smart phone and I showed Grandma Rose a video of a dog dressed in a silky robe with flowers on it. Two human arms were sticking out of the sleeves and it looked like the dog was eating breakfast with a spoon. Grandma started to laugh. After that, whenever she became upset we would show her a funny video. Most of the time it calmed her down and she became happy. This is called redirecting.

Those times were tough, but strangely, they were also good. We got to spend a lot of time with Grandma. Although her memories were fading, we were building good memories with her. When we were at school and Mom and Dad were at work, a care giver named Alicia came to the house and made sure Grandma Rose ate a good lunch and took her medicine. They went for walks, listened to music and did activities to help a little with her memory.

Stage 4: Moderate Decline – Symptoms are very clear and your loved one will have problems with simple arithmetic and paying their bills. They also start to forget things about their past.

In addition to forgetting to pay her bills, Grandma Rose would sometimes ask where Grandpa Charlie was although he had died several years earlier.

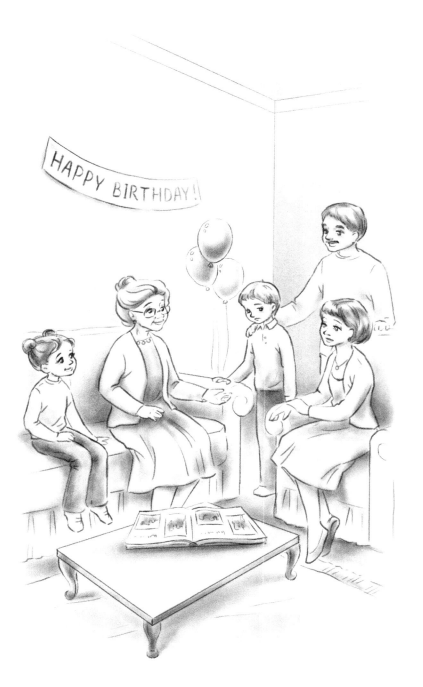

Chapter 6

It was April 20th – my ninth birthday. I already had a birthday party with all of my friends, but today we had invited family over for a barbeque and cupcakes. Some of our relatives had stopped visiting because they were sad that Grandma Rose had Alzheimer's, but they came today because it was my birthday.

I get it. Sometimes it's hard for me to be around her and see her going through this too, but you can't stop visiting someone just because you feel uncomfortable.

Most of our relatives looked familiar to her, and she remembered some of their names, but sometimes she didn't. This frustrated her. We brought out the old photo albums and we were surprised how much she remembered about "the good old days" when she was a young woman. It's strange that when you have Alzheimer's, you can't remember what you had for breakfast but you can often remember things that happened a long, long time ago.

All-in-all I think it was good for the relatives to see her. They weren't as scared as before even though they were still sad to see how confused she was.

Later, when we were cleaning up after the party, she told me that she had a good time with all of her nice new friends. She said, "I only wish my family could have been there for my birthday party." We laughed. I learned that you have to keep a sense of humor when dealing with someone with Alzheimer's. It's okay to smile find it humorous when they do something a little odd as long as you're not being cruel about it. Don't make fun of them if they're frustrated, but enjoy your time with them.

Stage 5: Moderately Severe – This is the stage when people get even more confused. The can usually take care of bathing and brushing their teeth, but may need to be reminded to do it. They need help with more and more of their daily activities.

They mostly remember their family and often talk about when they were young. It was actually fun hearing Grandma Rose talk about what it was like when she was a kid.

Chapter 7

In addition to having a poor memory, Grandma Rose was also getting weaker and it was harder for her to walk for very long. Her arthritis was bothering her more and she moved more slowly than she did just a couple years ago.

Whenever we could, we would take her out and do things that she enjoyed. She liked going out for coffee and donuts and then we would go shopping. We would bring along her transport chair in case she got tired. It's good to take your loved one out when you can.

One time, in the middle of the night, someone knocked loudly on our front door. When Dad opened it, there was a policeman with Grandma Rose standing next to him. She was in her night gown with the police officer's jacked draped over her shoulders, but she had nothing on her feet. It was quite cold and she had wandered from the house and gotten lost.

Thankfully she had a medical bracelet on her wrist that had her name and our address on it. She was very angry at the policeman and told him that she was just going back to her house and he didn't have any right to bring her to this place and leave her with people she didn't even know.

Another time she woke up very early and tried to make herself a cup of tea. She put the kettle on the stove, but it didn't have any water in it and it started a small fire in the kitchen. Thankfully the smoke detector went off and Dad was able to put it out.

Mom got a call from Alicia early one afternoon. Grandma Rose had hit her when Alicia tried to get her to take a shower. "Mrs. Harris," Alicia said, "I'm afraid that I won't be able to help her any more. Have you considered a memory care facility?"

After Grandma went to bed, we talked about what had happened and what needed to be done. The Alzheimer's was getting worse and since she had tried to hurt Alicia, Mom and Dad didn't feel that it was safe to have her stay at our house any more. It wasn't safe for her, and it might not be safe for us. What if she tried to make tea again, but didn't light the gas stove correctly? Or what if she accidentally started another fire?

Taking her to a memory care facility was the hardest decision my parents ever had to make, but they explained to us that Grandma needed to live in a place that was safe for her. There are people with a lot of training that would care for her all day and all night. Jake and I were really upset, but we knew that it was the right decision. I cried all night.

Just like we did when she moved into our house, we filled her room with the things she loved. We hung family pictures on the walls and, of course, put the beautiful quilt on her bed. Even though everyone was nice, and the place was neat and cheerful, it was sad seeing so many people, mostly women, walking up and down the hall like zombies. When we left, Mom and I cried. Dad and Jake didn't know what to do.

It was hard for Grandma Rose to adjust to living in the memory care facility. Everyone there was a stranger. They had a lot of activities that she liked to do, but it was challenging for the staff – there was always someone who was frustrated or angry.

The facility was close to our house so we were able to visit her ever couple of days. The staff did a great job of taking care of the residents, and I knew it was the right decision, but I hated seeing Grandma Rose so upset when we left. We were sad every time we walked out of the building.

Stage 6: Severe – This is a very hard stage and when things really began to get scary.

Your loved one won't be able to be left alone and will need help with everything. It's almost like they are a toddler again and they may have to wear an adult diaper because they don't realize they need to use the bathroom.

It was very hard for Mom and Dad to take her to a memory care facility, but it really was the best thing for her and for our family. Mom said she felt like a failure for not being able to care for Grandma Rose, but that's not true. Sometime the very best place for someone with dementia is with others who are trained to help them.

While she was still at our house Grandma Rose kept saying she wanted to "go home" and she was always confused. She also stopped telling us the stories of when she was young and most of the time just sat staring at the television.

No matter how hard it is, this is when they need you the most. Visit them as often as you can.

Chapter 8

A few times they had to send Grandma Rose to the hospital by ambulance because she was very sick. Each time that happened we were really scared. One day we got a call in the middle of the night that she had fallen out of bed and broken her shoulder. She was never really well after that. She hardly talked and would lay in her bed or sit hunched over in her wheelchair then fall asleep sitting there. Someone had to feed her and she couldn't care for herself at all.

Even though the staff at the memory care facility did their best, because she wasn't able to move very much, and had problems swallowing, she eventually got pneumonia and had to be taken to the hospital once more. The doctor said he was sorry, but this was the last stage of Alzheimer's Disease and all he could do was make sure she was comfortable until she passed away.

We knew this time would come, but it still felt like I was punched in the stomach. This is when I learned more new words, like hospice and palliative care. She was moved once more into a small hospice facility.

Hospice is a place that helps the patient and their family during this difficult time. They have a team of doctors, nurses and other very kind care givers. The team makes sure the patient is comfortable and a caregiver was almost always with her.

We held her hand, talked to her and played her favorite music. We weren't even sure that she knew we were there.

At hospice they didn't just help Grandma Rose, they also helped us. They prepared us for what would happen and made sure we had someone to talk to about our feelings. They laughed with us as we told great stories about Grandma Rose and hugged us when we were frightened.

Sometimes hospice care is given at home, but my parents thought having her in a facility would be better.

We did what we could to make her room nice. Once again we put the beautiful quilt she made many years ago on her bed. Jake and I drew pictures and put them on the wall.

No one can tell you how your loved one will be, but for her last few days, Grandma Rose just laid in bed with her eyes closed. She moaned like she was in pain, but the doctors had given her medicine.

I began to sing one of her favorite songs from church and then my Mom and Dad joined in. Jake was too shy to sing, but a strange thing happened . . . Grandma Rose stopped moaning and opened her eyes. It almost seemed like she knew who we were again – even if just for a short time.

We were all there and told her how much we loved her. My mom leaned over her, kissed her forehead and said, "We all love you so very much. When you feel it's time to go, don't be afraid. We're here with you." A few minutes later her nurse and doctor came in and she quietly slipped away.

Each person has a different experience when their loved one passes away and we were fortunate that it was so peaceful for Grandma Rose.

It isn't always like this – sometimes they are in a lot of pain or very frightened. We were afraid to leave the room because we didn't want her to be alone. One of the care givers said that sometimes the patient specifically waits for their family to leave the room before dying, and if this happened we shouldn't feel badly.

Stage 7: Very Severe – This is the final stage of Alzheimer's Disease and your loved one might be able to say a word or a phrase, but they can't really follow a conversation. Every once in a while Grandma Rose would say, "I want to go home."

The other word I told you about, palliative care . . . that means that the hospice staff makes sure your loved one is comfortable. The doctors and nurses give medications that will help with pain or help them relax if they are afraid. Other care givers might talk to the patient and gently give them a massage.

The staff was very caring and suggested different places where we could each get help. Hospice is not just for the patient, but helps the entire family.

Chapter 9

It's been a little over a year now, and like I said, I'm just now able to talk about it without crying. It takes some people a long time to grieve while others feel better in just a few weeks. There is no right way or wrong way to grieve and some people take a lot longer than others.

It's just very important to share your feelings with someone you trust and realize that the rest of your family will have different ways of processing their feelings.

At first I was mad at my brother Jake because he was always angry and yelled. My Dad made me realize that Jake wasn't really mad at us, he was just frustrated and frightened and sad but didn't know how to properly express it.

I don't want you to think that everything was always sad, and I hope you see in this story that even though there were a lot of sad times, there were also a lot of happy times. We made a lot of great memories and had a lot of great experiences throughout Grandma Rose's difficult journey with Alzheimer's.

It's strange, but I really learned a lot of interesting things about Grandma Rose that I might not have if she hadn't come to live with us or if I hadn't had to keep showing her the photo albums. Grandma Rose was really pretty when she was young, and she led a fascinating life.

She came from a large family and was the first one to graduate high school. Nowadays almost everyone graduates, but back during the Great Depression, people were very poor and kids left school around the 8th grade to go to work to help their families.

During World War II she went into the Women's Army Auxiliary Corps. It was really radical back then for a woman to join the military. She was stationed down South during the time of segregation. She and a friend were thrown off a bus for offering their seat to an African American woman with a baby.

Kids never think that their parents or grandparent were ever young, and Jake and I were amazed that Grandma Rose used to love to play baseball with her brothers and played on a team when she was in the Army. Or that she had to get out of the military when she married Grandpa Charlie because those were the rules back then.

Even if your grandparents don't have Alzheimer's Disease or dementia, you really should talk with them and see what things were like when they were young. They are living history books and have a lot of things they can teach us.

Anyway, I hope that if you are going through something similar, that this book has helped you understand a little better and that you won't be as scared as I was. I wish you peace on the really hard days and hope you find comfort knowing that there are others who have gone through the same thing as you are.

Love,
Carly

P.S. Grandma Rose's beautiful quilt is now on my bed and I snuggle in it every night and pretend she's giving me a big hug.

About the Author

Kim Roman is an Air Force "brat", an Air Force veteran, an Air Force wife, a home school mother, a world traveler and now an Oma to Katelyn, Luther and Reece. Her passion is teaching small-space, high-intensive organic gardening methods. As a Square Foot Gardening Certified Instructor (taught by Mel Bartholomew, the inventor of Square Foot Gardening) she supports the mission of the SFG Foundation which is to end world hunger. She is the owner of Square Foot Gardening 4 U and has a Facebook page by that name.

She and her daughter-in-law Crystal Falk, author of Sophia's Broken Crayons: A Story of Surrogacy from a Young Child's Perspective have created the Explain It To Me! - Sensitive Stories For Tough Topics series and more titles are on the way.

Made in the USA
Monee, IL
28 August 2022

12630208R00030